"Written from a place of personal pain and loss, *My Dwelling Place* points the reader to the only place of true comfort and protection—the presence of our Almighty God. In these captivating reflections from Psalm 91, Christa Mielke guides us through the meaning and application of perhaps familiar yet somewhat elusive descriptions of God as our shelter, our refuge, our dwelling place, and our deliverer in a way that will comfort our hearts and strengthen our faith, encouraging us to run to Him for safe harbor in the storms of life."

—Faith Taylor, Professor of Women's Ministries, Faith Baptist Bible College. Author: *A Look Within* and *Pray for Him*. BA, Local Church Ministries; MA, Biblical Studies.

"*My Dwelling Place* is a beautiful call to run to Jesus no matter what your season of life. Christa has captured the truth that King David experienced some two thousand years ago when he penned, "*In thy presence is fullness of joy; at thy right hand there are pleasures forevermore*" (Psalm 16:11, KJV). Her personal meditations have humbled my heart to "*Draw nigh to God, and he will draw nigh to you*" (James 4:8a, KJV), and I've learned what it means to abide under the pinion of Christ's wing. The journal's format is succinct, and the personal reflections stirred my heart to respond. This book is an invitation for your heart to walk in wisdom, encouragement, and faithful instruction and to grow in the knowledge of Jesus Christ: the name that is above every other name!"

—Cheryl Stitzinger, BS; MAC, women's ministry leader,
and counselor at Hope and Grace Counseling.
(hopeandgracecounsel@gmail.com)

"The contents of this book reveal one woman's journey through grief and loss to that place of freedom and joy found in submissively dwelling within the Lord's refuge. As I've read *My Dwelling Place*, the Lord has reminded me of His great and sovereign provision of all my needs. My heart rejoices and, as a result, has peace. May the Lord work in your heart as He has in mine, through Christa's vulnerable exposure of emotion and longing as she meditates on Psalm 91, pointing us to the beauty of dwelling in His shelter."

—Sonja Reimer, Revive Our Hearts Area Ambassador, MN,
Women's Bible study coordinator

"When we experience a crisis that threatens our physical wellbeing, we can dial 9-1-1, trusting that first responders will run to our aid with sirens blaring! When growing fear, painful loss, or unsettling doubt threaten to overwhelm our souls, we can go to 91:1 in the book of Psalms. Through careful meditation on the truth of this verse and each of the subsequent verses in this chapter, Christa gently urges us to seek peace and protection and to stay in the presence of the Most High—the only trustworthy and eternal source of refuge."

—Koryn R. Smith, PhD, Adjunct Faculty, Crown College, St. Bonifacius, MN

"In this unstable world with all the sorrows, grief, and heartaches we suffer, we often lose our focus on God and forget who He really is. Being a Ukrainian and going through a hard year for my nation and my entire family in Ukraine, this booklet became a great reminder that God is Almighty. I was so blessed by this verse-by-verse study of Psalm 91. It helped me to better understand what a privilege it is to abide and dwell in Him. He is my Refuge and my Fortress, my God, in whom I trust. I used *My Dwelling Place* for my personal study and with my family during our devotion time. It also worked great with our ladies' Bible study. I highly recommend this booklet."

—Luda O. S., Missionary to Central Asia

"In reading *My Dwelling Place*, you will feel with me as if Christa took our hands and ushered us into the serene and quiet peace of our home under the wings of God, *El Elyon*, under the shadow of *El Shaddai*. You too will be greatly comforted and instructed by her careful and insightful study of Psalm 91 as you walk with her through these stabilizing truths. Her thoughtful questions are most helpful for individual or group study. The results of the Word dwelling richly in Christa's soul will strengthen your heart!"

—Miriam Marriott, wife of the Chancellor of Maranatha Baptist University, host of weekly Bible classes, 'Girl Talk', and frequent speaker at women's events

my
dwelling
place

my dwelling place

Personal Meditations on Psalm 91
Christa Mielke

MY DWELLING PLACE
Copyright © 2023 by Christa Mielke

Cover/Interior Design: A special thanks to Amanda Mielke, who created the original cover design, which inspired the final design. (https://cuethedesign.com/)

Author Photo: Pastor Justus Schofield

All Scripture quotations, unless otherwise indicated, are taken from the Holy Bible, English Standard Version. Copyright © 2000, 2001 by Crossway Bibles, a division of Good News Publishers. Used by Permission. All rights reserved. • Scripture quotations marked (KJV) are taken from the King James Version of the Bible, which is in the public domain.

ISBN: 978-1-4866-2425-6
eBook ISBN: 978-1-4866-2426-3

Word Alive Press
119 De Baets Street Winnipeg, MB R2J 3R9
www.wordalivepress.ca

WORD ALIVE
—P R E S S—

Cataloguing in Publication information can be obtained from Library and Archives Canada.

Dedicated To:

DANIEL, YOU ARE my leader, my lover, and my laughter. Thank you for always pointing me back to my true shelter and joy. I see Jesus in you. Thank you for encouraging me and leading me to greater heights of glory with God.

Marcus, Matthias, and Katiyanna, I am eternally grateful for the privilege of being your mother. You are more precious to me than life itself. Thank you for loving me despite my flaws, and for the beautiful ways you remind me of God and His love. I pray that you learn to make the Most High your dwelling place and truly abide in His shadow.

Tikvah, תִּקְוָה, my precious child I never met but deeply love, thank you for how you have taught and continue to teach me to run to my true Shelter. You have been an instrument of my sanctification and a purifier of my worship. I'm so thankful you are safe in the arms of Jesus. I will meet you someday. Until then, "*The* LORD *gave, and the* LORD *has taken away; blessed be the name of the* LORD" (Job 1:21).[1]

The Lord Jesus Christ. Thank you so much for being "*my refuge and my fortress, my God, in whom I trust*" (Psalm 91:2). My life is yours, and I want to reflect your steadfast love and the living hope you have given me. Thank you for Calvary and the gospel glory that redeems my sin and pain for your eternal purposes.

---

1 See also "Heaven Someday," Shelly E. Johnson, accessed April 20, 2023, https://shellyejohnson.com/videos/.

Dear Reader,

WELCOME TO MY journal. I'm so glad you've decided to join me in studying Psalm 91. What's recorded on the following pages isn't intended to be a thorough discourse but simply the overflow of much time spent lingering, praying, studying, and weeping through this Psalm.

In 2021 my husband and I experienced a devastating miscarriage. This occurred after six years of trying for another child. God said, "No." My heart was broken and my faith was struggling. In 2022 I attended a conference where I was challenged to participate in a "Holy Girl Walk." This involved getting out and walking every day for one month. While walking, I was to memorize and meditate on Psalm 91. What began as a spiritual and physical exercise turned into an encounter with God on a deeply personal level. While continuing to walk through the lingering pain, I began to meditate on Psalm 91. I nestled closer to Him, and I found Him to be true to His Word and His nature. The promise of future hope began to take formation in the present as I sheltered under His wings, secure behind the shield of His faithfulness.

I don't know what sorrows and fears God may have allowed to come your way, but I do know the God who has allowed them. I pray that as you linger longer on the truths in Psalm 91, you begin to breathe again with revived hope as you have a renewed view of the Most High God.

All for Jesus, Christa Mielke, Psalm 73:25–26

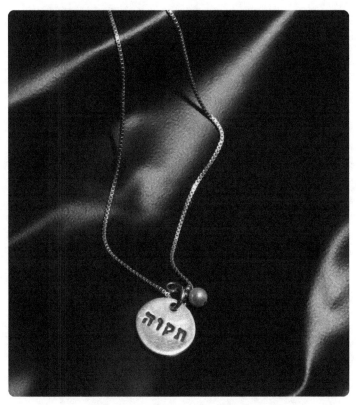

Tikvah, תִּקְוָה, is the name of our precious little one, who is now
safe in the arms of Jesus. It means a cord of hope. Just as Rahab
wound herself tightly around the person and promises of God,
let down her tikvah, and placed her hope in God,
so do I!

Thank you, Laura Johansen, for the gift of this necklace.

Acknowledgments

SPECIAL THANKS TO:

Daniel Mielke—Thank you, my husband, for always showing me Jesus. Thank you for patiently walking alongside me in my grief, even as you grieve. You are such an excellent daddy, and I know you would have been just as excellent with our Tikvah. I value your many labors contributing to this book's completion and your gentle shepherding in our home throughout this entire process.

Dannah Gresh—I will forever be thankful that I was able to attend the True Woman Conference in 2022 and hear your challenge to participate in a Holy Girl Walk. I didn't know I needed to spend such a saturated amount of time in Psalm 91. Your transparency and humility concerning your struggles and what God had been teaching you through this beautiful Psalm urged me to investigate. Thank you for allowing God to take you through hardships and for using those hardships as platforms for gospel glory.

Faith Taylor—Thank you for investing in my personal growth, encouraging me to publish, and contributing to the polishing of *My Dwelling Place*. I will never forget the phone call we shared a short time after Tikvah went to Heaven. You sat with me in my grief and taught me to think longer and surrender to God's goodness. Thank you for patiently helping me sort through my emotions and questions and for always pointing me back to Jesus. Your words are always reinforced by scripture and gentle care. Thank you for being a truth teller in my life. I am deeply grateful for you.

Pastor Justus Schofield—You were my brother first, then my friend, and then my pastor. Hasn't God been so kind to us? Thank you for adopting a new role—that of my photographer. You have jumped through so many hoops just for me on so many occasions, and I value your servant-heart, humble spirit, and excellent product. Thank you for loving me and being a godly man whom I respect.

Grace Baptist Church, Austin, Minnesota—You have walked alongside the Mielke family amid great loss. Thank you for loving us so well and pointing us to Jesus. We love you all and deeply value the privilege of experiencing life's joys, sorrows, and ministries together. Thank you for your support and encouragement.

Amanda Mielke (cuethedesign.com)—Thank you for helping me with the first printing. You were invaluable, and your eye for detail was excellent. You're a talented designer and a wonderful sister-in-love!

Editing Team—Thank you to those who edited my book for the first printing. Your labors were part of my refinement and growth. I appreciate your friendship.

All for Jesus,

Christa M. Mielke

Psalm 91:1—16

He who dwells in the shelter of the Most High will abide in the shadow of the Almighty. I will say to the LORD, "My refuge and my fortress, my God, in whom I trust." For he will deliver you from the snare of the fowler and from the deadly pestilence. He will cover you with his pinions, and under his wings you will find refuge; his faithfulness is a shield and buckler.

You will not fear the terror of the night, nor the arrow that flies by day, nor the pestilence that stalks in darkness, nor the destruction that wastes at noonday. A thousand may fall at your side, ten thousand at your right hand, but it will not come near you. You will only look with your eyes and see the recompense of the wicked. Because you have made the LORD your dwelling place— the Most High, who is my refuge—no evil shall be allowed to befall you, no plague come near your tent. For he will command his angels concerning you to guard you in all your ways. On their hands they will bear you up, lest you strike your foot against a stone. You will tread on the lion and the adder; the young lion and the serpent you will trample underfoot.

"Because *he holds fast to me in love, I will deliver him; I will protect him, because he knows my name. When he calls to me, I will answer him; I will be with him in trouble; I will rescue him and honor him. With long life I will satisfy him and show him my salvation.*" (emphasis added)

Psalm 91:1

> "He who dwells in the shelter of
> the Most High will abide in the
> shadow of the Almighty."

WHAT DOES IT mean to dwell and abide? The shadow of the Almighty, the very near presence of *El Shaddai*, holds a promise of protection and safety. This promise, however, is conditional. The shelter of the Lord Most High, the shadow of the Almighty, is available to all but only accessible to those who choose to dwell.

To dwell means to inhabit, to take up residence. It means to make the presence of God the place one chooses to be. The terms "to dwell" and "abide" are similar in meaning. A finer nuance of the word "abide" is to remain. Abide means to stay—I do not leave. If I truly dwell in His presence, I won't want to or need to depart.

Even when I can't identify, quantify, or rectify the realities of life, I can hunker down and press in to stay. The psalmist's point here is that if I go under God's protection and stay there, I will be in the very near presence of the *One* who is above all things. There is nothing higher than *El Elyon*, the Lord Most High. No one holds more authority or power. No one has a greater right to rule. No one else owns or deserves this lofty and exalted title. He holds all might, and everything—everything—is under Him, bows to Him, can't escape Him, and is within His ability and right to direct and control. Absolutely nothing usurps His headship. This is a place of true shelter and covering.

Notice the words of covering used in this psalm: shelter, shadow (v. 1), pinons, wings, shield, buckler (v. 4), guard (v. 11). Think about it: He is the Lord Most High, the Almighty; therefore, His coverage never fails. He never leaves gaping holes and never fails to fully protect those who enter His shadow. He is all-encompassing. When I choose to reside in His covering, I choose the only place of true refuge. However, I must dwell; I must abide.

When I know who He is and what He can do, why would I not run to Him and allow Him to cover me? Even the strongest storms and greatest battles of my life can't remove His covering. Whatever I'm facing, He will not leave me defenseless. If I stay under His care, I, and the watching world, will see Him as He has revealed Himself to be—*El Elyon, El Shaddai.*

Personal Reflections

1. Write out Psalm 91:1.

_____

_____

_____

_____

_____

2. How does pondering the meaning of El Elyon and El Shaddai
   impact my desire and ability to dwell and abide?

_____

_____

_____

_____

_____

3. Because nothing is higher than God, and everything is under
   Him, how do arrogance or ignorance come into play when I
   seek shelter elsewhere?

_____

_____

_____

_____

_____

4. What are possible reasons why I don't abide in His shelter?

_____

_____

_____

_____

_____

5. What are practical ways I can abide in the shadow of the Almighty?

_____

_____

_____

_____

_____

Psalm 91:1–2

> "He who dwells in the shelter of
> the Most High will abide in the
> shadow of the Almighty. I will say
> to the LORD, 'My refuge, and my
> fortress, my God in whom I trust.'"

I AM ASTOUNDED by how accessible God has made Himself. He's described as the shelter of the Most High and the shadow of the Almighty. When I'm in His shelter, I'm in His shadow, in the very near presence of God. This is a sacred place—astoundingly, mercifully, and gratefully open and available to me. It signifies the reality that God's battle is not *with* me but *for* me. I'm no longer His enemy. I have direct access (Hebrews 4:16). Beyond this, I'm on His side. Therefore, He takes responsibility for my care. He will protect me if I simply run to Him for refuge. When I run to the fortress, I have unhindered access to the Almighty, Most High King Himself. While He does employ others to protect and help me (as seen later in Psalm 91), He Himself is my refuge and my fortress, *my* God in whom I trust! When *Someone* with such authority and might makes Himself available as a place of shelter and refuge, why would I not trust Him? Why would I fail to run into God's loving, waiting arms of refuge.[2]

Too often my natural response is to listen to myself rehearse life's hardships. I look inward instead of upward. The agonies seem heavy, and at times they're all I can see. However, the psalmist models a better path. He purposefully lifts his eyes to behold his God and talk to himself about these truths. I'm sure he didn't always feel those truths, but feelings follow faith, and as he ran to his God, he found shelter.

I'm struck by the fact that verse 2 doesn't say, "And the Lord said to me, 'I am your refuge, and my fortress, my God in whom I trust.'" The psalmist says he will tell this to the Lord. This trust is convicting. He's not trying to coax and convince himself into trust. This is the psalmist talking to God with a statement of confidence and surrender: "You are these things, and I am affirming and aligning my heart to these realities."

Sometimes, even in telling myself truth, I can exclude talking to God, and I end up trying to *work* myself into an acknowledgment of who God is instead of *surrender* myself there. Both are a choice. One choice is my strength; the other is His. I want to run to Him today in surrender, affirming and aligning my heart to the reality of Who He is and how these truths impact my trust. These verses are both comforting and

---

2 "Take Shelter," Getty Music, accessed May 18, 2023, https://store.gettymusic.com/us/song/take- shelter/.

convicting: comforting to consider that God would do this for me, and convicting because of how frequently I fail to run to Him.

Personal Reflections

1. Write out Psalm 91:2.

_____

_____

_____

_____

_____

2. What is my pattern? Do I listen to myself rehearse the struggle over and over, or do I counsel myself with the truth?

_____

_____

_____

_____

_____

3. Does the fact that God is *for* me influence my running to Him for refuge? If not, why?

_____

_____

_____

_____

_____

4. What is the difference between working and surrendering my
   way to an acknowledgment of who God is?

_____

_____

_____

_____

_____

5. How would I know if I was living by faith or feelings?

_____

_____

_____

_____

_____

Psalm 91:3

> "For He will deliver you from the
> snare of the fowler and from the
> deadly pestilence."

(A snare is activated by the victim's
own momentum forward.)[3]

I AM BEING hunted, observed, weighed, enticed, and pursued. My weaknesses are exploited, and my strengths are used against me. My appetites easily fool me and draw me into the snare the hunter has laid. As the bait awaits my pursuit, the hunter awaits my own momentum forward. The pursuit of my passion ensnares me. Suddenly, I realize I'm trapped! I begin to struggle and fight against my entrapment. I struggle with all my might to obtain freedom from my deceptive and self-inflicted bondage.

3 Inspired by Dannah Gresh, "Inviting Heaven to Rule in Your Mind," September 23, 2022, found in "Events," Revive Our Hearts, accessed May 1, 2023, https://www.reviveourhearts.com/events/true-woman-22/inviting-heaven-rule-your-mind/.

The struggle simply intensifies the snare. I am incapable of freeing myself. I need outside deliverance.

"*He will deliver you from the snare of the fowler*" (v. 3, emphasis added). My Deliverer comes to me with knife drawn and gentleness in His eyes, yet I withdraw from His touch. I must get free; I must do it myself. I got myself into this mess; I will get myself out. He compassionately tells me, "I will deliver you from the snare of the fowler" (v. 3).

I immediately realize what I must do. I must stop fighting, stop questioning, stop squirming, and stop resisting. I must rest in what He's doing to cut me free. This process is terrifying! I might be asked to turn and become uncomfortable in order to give Him access to my pain, but He is skilled and compassionate, and *He* will do it ... *not me*. I can contribute nothing to my deliverance except the surrender and obedience to allow it. *He* will deliver me.

Personal Reflections

1. Write out Psalm 91:3.

_____

_____

_____

_____

_____

2. What snares have entangled me?

_____

_____

_____

_____

_____

3. In what ways have I endeavored to free myself?

_____

_____

_____

_____

_____

4. What thoughts about God hinder me from accepting His offer of deliverance?

_____

_____

_____

_____

_____

5. What steps of obedience would I need to take in order to accept God's deliverance?

_____

_____

_____

_____

_____

Psalm 91:4

> "He will cover you with His pinions, and under His wings you will find refuge; his faithfulness is a shield and buckler."

THE WORD "COVER" is captivating. To be covered by His wings implies a nearness to the *one* covering, a sheltering from the onslaught of the trial that surrounds. There, in the safety of His covering, the sorrows of life lose their power and ability to violate the hope within my soul. It doesn't mean the storm has ceased, but it implies a place of refuge and safety amid the storm.

What is necessary to *be* covered? First, I must come under. I must go there. I can't expect covering apart from my willingness to allow Him to cover me. He says, "He *will*." Will I let Him? Second, there must be a willingness to surrender and stay (dwell, abide, as in v. 1) in that covering. To be covered with His pinions, under His wings, is to be right up next to Him. This is not a covering absent of His presence. No! This is an invitation, a promise of covering that includes God's active presence and personal involvement. When I am covered by Him, I am in the very near presence of *El Elyon*!

This draws my mind to my sweet, young daughter. She has a tender spirit and is easily scared when we're watching a family film. Often, something we might not consider to be terrifying has her begging me to take my very warm blanket and cover her face so that she doesn't have to endure the scene. As a mother who loves her daughter, I eagerly respond to this request as she continues to ask me, "Is it over? Is it over? When will it be over? Do you know what you're doing?" I smile as I gently remind her that I will protect her.

However, my daughter also has a need to know ... a need to understand. (She may or may not get this from her mother.) So while I'm covering her, I'll notice my sweet daughter peeking around the covering of the blanket with one eye covered and the other on the screen, needing to see for herself, uncertain of my ability to both protect and know what to do. Instead of confidently resting in my covering, she anxiously and frantically experiences the trauma with a pseudo sense of protection.

How like my own heart. So often I have run to God for refuge, but I keep doubting Him: "Is it over, God? Is it over? When will it be over? Do you know what you're doing?" Then, peeking out at the storm, not in anticipation of the powerful working of my Protector over the storm but with a need to comprehend, I look at the storm through my understanding and expectations, forgetting *Who* is covering me.

I often try to make sure I'm truly being protected, as if somehow my involvement may be necessary, or that my trepidation, which caused me to run under His wings in the first place, can now rise above and meet the challenge better than the One I supposedly ran to. This is why the psalmist draws attention to the character of God: "His *faithfulness is a shield and buckler.*" If He wasn't faithful and powerful, His protection would be insufficient. Nevertheless, He is faithful and true. Therefore, His complete covering is certain. The protection He offers is as sure as His character.

However, His covering is only as effective as my willingness to stay under. How much better it is to nestle myself close to His heart, not oblivious of the troubles but deeply aware of Him ... not merely anticipating the end of the struggle but eagerly anticipating His glorious, purposeful, and timely victory over the struggle!

> His covering is only as effective as my willingness to stay under.

He will cover you ...

Personal Reflections

1. Write out Psalm 91:4.

_____

_____

_____

_____

_____

2. Which is true of me: I need to *come* under His covering, or *stay* under His covering? Explain.

_____

_____

_____

_____

_____

3. Do I find myself peeking out from under His covering?

_____

_____

_____

_____

_____

4. Does my life reveal that I believe God can protect me and will, or does it demonstrate my need for control?

_____

_____

_____

_____

_____

5. How does God's faithfulness as a shield and buckler impact my confidence in His protection?

_____

_____

_____

_____

_____

Psalm 91:5—6

> "You will not fear the terror of the night, nor the arrow that flies by day, nor the pestilence that stalks in darkness, nor the destruction that wastes at noonday."

IT'S IN THE noise and reality of the battle that God equips my heart not to fear. When life is swirling all around me, it doesn't have to swirl within me. If I'm abiding, dwelling under His wings, I will experience the complete protection His faithfulness provides (v. 4). God will not abandon me and cannot be conquered. Therefore, in the shadow of the Almighty ... I will not fear.

This in no way diminishes the struggle's reality. The battle is *still* being waged. There is *still* a real terror of the night, the arrow is *still* flying, the pestilence is *still* stalking, and destruction is *still* wasting! While the *still* continues, I can be still in the shelter of the Almighty. He is there, taking the brunt of it all while I nestle in His care. He is the *One* facing and fighting the battle. Because He is the Lord Most High, the Almighty, I can rest. Nothing can outmaneuver Him or thwart Him. Because of His faithfulness, I am truly and eternally safe.

The reality of who He is and my proximity and relationship to Him grant me the ability to say, "I will not fear, even while the circumstances are raging!" I don't need the trial to cease, the desire to be fulfilled, or the circumstance to change to be at peace, at rest. I need only run to His shelter and stay there, confident in Who *He* is. *What* is coming at me or *when* it comes is insignificant. The *form* or *time* of the trial are never qualifiers for my peace. Nothing comes at me that He can't handle ... at *any* time, day or night. As certain as the reality of the trial might be, even more certain is the power and ability of God to combat it and give me freedom from fear. When I choose to know and remain in my Protector's care, I can choose not to fear.

Personal Reflections

1. Write out Psalm 91:5–6.

_____

_____

_____

_____

_____

2. Do I believe that I shouldn't have to face trouble in this life? Why?

_____

_____

_____

_____

_____

3. Is my life characterized by fear? If yes, how?

_____

_____

_____

_____

_____

4. In what way does the *form* or *time* of the trial currently impact my response?

_____

_____

_____

_____

_____

5. How does laying my fear down require active rest?

_____

_____

_____

_____

_____

Psalm 91:7–8

> "A thousand may fall at your side,
> ten thousand at your right hand,
> but it will not come near you. You
> will only look with your eyes and
> see the recompense of the wicked."

GOD NEVER PROMISED believers that they wouldn't experience sorrow, sickness, or strife. Remember verses 5–6? The terror of the night is still there, the arrow is still flying, the pestilence is still stalking, and the destruction is still wasting. Believers will experience the tragedy and trauma of living in a sin-sick world. No one is exempt from the reality of the curse. Every believer can attest to having faced hardship.

What's happening in these verses is something entirely different. The reason the thousands and ten thousand are falling is that they're under God's wrath. These particular people are experiencing judgment because they're outside of God's shelter.

They have tried to live independently of God, and they can't stand against His might and authority.

The word "recompense" indicates negative reward or retribution. As a born again believer, I will look and see the judgment of unbelievers, but I will *only* look and see. I will *not* experience it! This is an awful reality for those apart from Jesus. My heart should be moved with compassion and motivated to share Christ's love with them. Indeed, this truth is terrifyingly sad, but their fall has no bearing upon my personal standing in Christ: "*There is therefore now no condemnation to those who are in Christ Jesus*" (Romans 8:1). What amazing grace! What an incredible shelter! I will experience trials and tribulations, but it will not be because I am under God's wrath. I have a living hope (see 1 Peter 1:1–9). I am protected, and the same strength and power that is angry with the wicked every day is shielding me in love.

Personal Reflections

1. Write out Psalm 91:7–8.

_____

_____

_____

_____

_____

2. How have I experienced both the consequences of living in a sin-cursed world and the consequences of my own sin?

_____

_____

_____

_____

_____

3. Am I under God's wrath? Do I really know Jesus as my Lord and Savior?

_____

_____

_____

_____

_____

4. As a believer, have I "gotten over" being sheltered from God's wrath?

_____

_____

_____

_____

_____

5. Is my heart moved with proactive compassion for those under God's wrath?

_____

_____

_____

_____

_____

Psalm 91:9–10

> "Because you have made the LORD
> your dwelling place—the Most
> High, who is my refuge—no evil
> shall be allowed to befall you, no
> plague come near your tent."

THE CONTINUING CONTRAST of the wicked and those who have run to God for shelter is filled with a powerful return to the truths in verses 1–2. As the psalmist reflects on the recompense of the wicked, he directs his attention back to *Jehovah, El Elyon.* The reason I won't experience the recompense of the wicked in verses 7–8 is because the Lord is my dwelling place. Lest I begin to imagine I have accomplished my deliverance, the psalmist reminds me of *Jehovah,* the self-existent One who is *El Elyon,* the Most High God. Lest I believe my efforts have bought my safety, lest I assume my wisdom or merits have been or could ever be my refuge, the psalmist reiterates the Person of Refuge, the Place of Refuge, the Practice of Refuge, the Proof of Refuge, and the Promise of Refuge.

The <u>Person of Refuge</u>, the self-existent *One* who is Most High, needs no one to sustain or strengthen Him. He offers His limitless support and strength to all who come to Him.

The <u>Place of Refuge</u> is the Person of Refuge, "*your dwelling place.*" They are the same. I typically think of a place as a location, from one common noun to another. However, in this instance, the location is the proper noun of God Himself.

The <u>Practice of Refuge</u> is the intentional, positional, relational, and habitual choosing to make *Jehovah*, *El Elyon*, my refuge, "*because* <u>*you have made*</u> the LORD *your dwelling place*" (emphasis added). In order to find refuge, I must *go* to where He is and *remain.*

The <u>Proof of Refuge</u> is evidenced through the psalmist. He wants his readers to know that this Person of Refuge is a proven refuge, and he provides the proof through his testimony.

> The one who runs to the true Refuge will not have reason to fear and will have the absolute protective covering of the Most High.

I can hear his excitement as he seemingly blurts out, "The Most High ... He is my refuge too ... I've seen Him. I know Him. He has covered me too. I testify and declare to you He is who He says He is and will do what He says He will do."

The <u>Promise of Refuge</u> is contingent upon the practice of running to the proven Person and Place of Refuge. "... *no evil shall be allowed to befall you, no plague come near your tent.*" The one who runs to the true Refuge will not have reason to fear and will have the absolute protective covering of the Most High. He is a trustworthy faithful God. I can take Him at His Word.

The questions lingering underneath these powerful truths are, "Have I made the Lord my dwelling place? If so, am I remaining there?"

Personal Reflections

1. Write out Psalm 91:9–10.

_____

_____

_____

_____

_____

2. How does reflecting on the Person and Place of Refuge stabilize my heart?

_____

_____

_____

_____

_____

3. What is my practice for refuge? Do I make the Lord my dwelling place? If not, where do I typically go?

_____

_____

_____

_____

_____

4. When in my life has God proven He is indeed my refuge?

_____

_____

_____

_____

_____

5. Is there a part of me that believes God lied to me about His protection? Why?

_____

_____

_____

_____

_____

Psalm 91:9—10

> "Because you have made the LORD
> your dwelling place—the Most
> High, who is my refuge—no evil
> shall be allowed to befall you, no
> plague come near your tent."

THE PROMISE OF Refuge from verse 10, "*no evil shall be allowed to befall you, no plague come near your tent,*" presents my heart with pause. How do I reconcile this promise with the deeply painful and even desperately wicked realities I face? It seems that evil does befall me and the plague does come near my tent. Clarity comes in understanding the word "evil" as being qualitatively different from the word "affliction." I will go through trials in this life. I will experience the sinfulness of this world, and it may even encroach upon the door of my home, but this is where the promise activates. No *evil*! What I face in this life is only ever allowed by the hand of the Most High, so when I experience the trials of life, they are for good, not evil.

The realities of life demand clarification. How do I reconcile a good God and the pain that surrounds and abounds? Ben Flegal brought out this tension in a message he shared as he reflected upon the loss of his wife: "We must not slander the character of God by calling good what He calls evil."[4] The reality of sin and its consequences are *not* good. This is the gospel imperative. Jesus died because I'm in a world fraught with sin, so I will experience the side effects of this reality.

One of the victories Jesus purchased through His resurrection was deliverance from a broken world that suffers under the weight of sin's consequences. The Almighty God, *El Shaddai*, The Most High, *El Elyon* is able to deliver and uses sin and its consequences for my good. He is a transforming God. He Himself never changes, yet He is able to change people and circumstances for His glory and purposes. I live in a world cursed by sin. Consequently, it's not the *reality* of the situation that is good. Goodness is found as a *result* of who God is and how God uses the realities I face.

This foundational truth highlights to me that it is good for me to experience the situations He allows. He uses the consequences of my living in a sin-sick world to purify, preserve, and posture me for His glory. Scripture reminds me of His good and loving hand working in me "*a far more exceeding and eternal weight of glory*" (2 Corinthians 4, KJV). This brings to mind what Joseph said in a seemingly evil situation: "*As for you, you meant evil against me, but God meant it for good*" (Genesis 50:20a). This

---

4 Maranatha Baptist University, "MBU Chapel: Ben Flegal," YouTube, October 18, 2022, 57:05, https://www.youtube.com/watch?v=u3DbZgNy34M.

is the transforming work of God: purpose *for* and power *in* my pain.

When I experience the arrows and the plagues of this life, it's not the punishment of God nor a vile corruption that only serves to debase and demoralize—that would be evil. I can rest assured that when God allows something to seemingly slip through the covering of His wings, it was indeed faithfulness that allowed its entrance. Nothing can touch me unless God allows it. Remember, "*no evil shall be <u>allowed</u> to befall you*" (emphasis added). This indicates that everything that touches my life, even in the most secret places of my heart, is *allowed* by God, and therefore it *becomes* good.

The shield and buckler of His faithfulness (v. 4) continues to guard and protect me because it is His faithfulness that *allowed* the struggle to come at all. "*I know, O LORD, that your rules are righteous, and that in faithfulness you have afflicted me. Let your steadfast love comfort me according to your promise to your servant*" (Psalm 119:75–76). "*Because (I) have made the LORD (my) dwelling place—the Most High, who is my refuge—no evil shall be allowed to befall (me), no plague come near (my) tent.*" It is true then. I can rest.

Personal Reflections

1. Write out Psalm 91:9–10.

_____

_____

_____

_____

_____

2. What is the difference between evil and affliction, and what is God's role in that difference?

_____

_____

_____

_____

_____

3. How or why is Ben Flegal's statement about slandering God appropriate and necessary in times of sorrow and grief?

_____

_____

_____

_____

_____

4. Can I claim or expect that I will not face sickness, war, trials, etc. because of this verse? Why or why not (hint: v. 7, 15)?

_____

_____

_____

_____

_____

5. How do the faithfulness of God and the allowance of God in Psalm 119:75–76 challenge my current perspective of the struggles I'm facing?

_____

_____

_____

_____

_____

Psalm 91:11–12

> "For he will command his angels
> concerning you to guard you in all
> your ways. On their hands they
> will bear you up, lest you strike
> your foot against a stone."

THE REASON NO evil will befall me and no plague will come near my tent is because I have made the Lord my dwelling place. When I shelter in Him, *Jehovah* takes active measures to protect me. As *El Elyon*, the armies of the hosts of heaven are at His disposal, and He mobilizes them.

Have I fully considered that my name was on the lips of God in a commissioning charge to the Hosts of Heaven on my behalf? Do I recognize the reality that God Himself protects me and shelters me, and part of His protection includes the angels? Their mission? To guard me, to keep and protect me. *All* my ways are covered by the shield and buckler of God's faithfulness (v. 7) and His messengers. This is an encompassing reality—not some

> Have I fully considered that my name was on the lips of God in a commissioning charge to the Hosts of Heaven on my behalf?

of my ways, but all of my ways. The angels, charged with my care, uphold me, bear me up, and guard me against evils big and small.

A small-scale comparison might be to imagine myself captured in enemy territory, and as I'm an American citizen, the President of the United States mobilizes one of the most elite military forces known to time and history, the Navy Seals. How would this knowledge change my perspective? Wouldn't I be filled hope, gratitude, and positional awe?

How much more should my heart swell with the knowledge that God has deployed His elite for my protection? Out of all the people on the earth who have ever been, or ever will be, God knows my name, location, need, and struggles—and so do His angels.

It can't be said that the God of Heaven Who spoke and the universe began, Who formed and holds planets in their orbit, Who forged the mountains, Who scooped out the depths of the oceans, Who breathed life into humanity, Who saw the depravity of humanity and sent His only Son Jesus to suffer, die, and rise again, Who conquered sin, death, and hell, Who gives the Spirit of God to be my Helper, Who wrote the Word to reveal Himself to me, Who has given many kindnesses and blessings, and Who also employs the armies of heaven to defend and guard His children now has a chink in His armor or a weakness in His defensive line. Absolutely nothing can break through this kind of power and love. The forces of Hell are immobilized when His forces are energized.

When I walk through the harrowing realities of life, it is not because God lied or failed. Rather, it's because God, in His sovereign goodness, opened the door and granted access. Since His faithfulness allowed it, whatever it is, it is good for me to be afflicted (see Psalm 119:71).

Wait! It was God Who actively opened the defensive line and allowed my miscarriage, and it's good for me?

Indeed. He did.

Indeed. It is.

Do I really know Who He is? Do I really understand how He operates? The confusing and painful truth of God's active involvement in my sorrow is only comforting if I know and accept that God is Who He has revealed Himself to be throughout this psalm: *Jehovah* (The LORD), *El Elyon* (Most High), *El Shaddai* (Almighty), *Elohim* (my God). When God opens the defensive line and allows an arrow to embed, a pestilence to hit, or a stone to strike, it's because in His faithfulness to His own nature there are greater realities at play than simply the struggle itself.

Personal Reflections

1. Write out Psalm 91:11–12.

_____

_____

_____

_____

_____

2. Why should knowing that God has commissioned His angels with my care bring me comfort?

_____

_____

_____

_____

_____

3. Do I believe that all my ways are guarded by God and His angels, or is there a part of me that supposes God has a chink in His armor?

_____

_____

_____

_____

_____

4. When it feels like I'm not sheltered, what truths must I use to counter my feelings?

_____

_____

_____

_____

_____

5. What God-ordained circumstances do I need to surrender to His eternal picture?

_____

_____

_____

_____

_____

Psalm 91:13

> "You will tread upon the lion and
> the adder; the young lion you will
> trample underfoot."

I CAN HEAR a victory cry ringing across human existence as this verse reminds me of the One who has truly conquered all. Since the fall, humanity has waited eagerly for the One, the Messiah, who would crush the head of the enemy underfoot. The Lord God, speaking to the serpent, Satan, said, "I will put enmity between you and the woman, and between your offspring and her offspring; he shall bruise your head, and you shall bruise his heel" (Genesis 3:15). Jesus, the promised Conqueror and Deliverer, did indeed come, and He did indeed deal a death blow to the Serpent, the Devil. Here in Psalm 91, the psalmist is captivated by the promise of refuge and what this refuge truly entails.

Throughout time, battles waged have often had places of refuge, which would hold only until the wall was broken through or the resources within the fortress were depleted. In such cases, the refuge was temporary, fleeting, and eventually it would become a tomb. However, this is not so with the Most High, "*Who is my refuge*" (v. 9). When I run to Him, the safety and protection He offers is not a postponement of inevitable defeat. The psalmist instead seems to call to mind Messiah's promised victory over Satan. Christ wins, and it doesn't matter what tactics Satan uses to thwart God, because he cannot gain the upper hand.

A serpent or snake is extremely deceptive and sly, often camouflaged by its surroundings and lightning fast as it strikes its prey. A lion, especially a young, powerful lion, is bold, on the prowl, and uses its fierceness to intimidate and strike terror into the heart of its target. Both methods of hunting are extremely effective and employed by my enemy. This is why 1 Peter 5:8 warns, "*Be sober-minded; be watchful. Your adversary the devil prowls around like a roaring lion, seeking someone to devour.*"

Hope and victory don't come by believing Satan has no power and is not a terrifying foe. Hope and victory come by acknowledging how vicious and cunning he is while simultaneously acknowledging that this is insignificant. He is no match for God. And here, struggling heart, lies the building blocks of hope. Because *Jehovah* is my dwelling place when He wins—I *win*! I

> Because Jehovah is my dwelling place when He wins—I win! I am positionally postured for victory because I am with the victor!

am positionally postured for victory because I am *with the victor*! The final battle is already decided. As a believer in Jesus Christ, I conquer because He conquered: "No, *in all these things we are more than conquerors through him who loved us*" (Romans 8:37). If I will only abide with the Conquering King, I don't have to give up the skirmishes along the way. His resources for victory are immeasurable.

Whatever foe strategically battles against me, it is certainly powerless unless I give it power. This is true regardless of how cunning or frightening the foe is, regardless of its size or strength, regardless of whether it's the work of the enemy or even the deceitfulness of my sin (see James 1:14–15). If I abide, I will tread and trample victoriously, because the victor of all has claimed and imparted victory to those who abide.

In Christ, I cannot lose the ultimate battle, but I can give up ground to the enemy by failing to stay close to the victor. I want to reclaim any ground lost by clinging to Jesus and allowing Him to equip me for victorious battle (see 2 Peter 1:3–4).

Personal Reflections

1. Write out Psalm 91:13.

_____

_____

_____

_____

_____

2. Has the victory of Jesus ceased to empower my daily walk? If yes, in what ways?

_____

_____

_____

_____

_____

3. How have I fallen prey to Satan's boldness or cunningness?

_____

_____

_____

_____

_____

4. What do my continual failures reveal about my understanding of God's ability to give me victory and/or my understanding of how to appropriate His immeasurable resources?

_____

_____

_____

_____

_____

5. Have I lost any ground? How can I, by God's power, reclaim this territory? What active steps of dependence should I take?

_____

_____

_____

_____

_____

Psalm 91:14

> "Because he holds fast to me in
> love, I will deliver him;
> I will protect him, because he
> knows my name."

THE PSALMIST HAS been declaring all the ways in which God will protect and cover those who come under Him for protection. He's been talking to himself about the truths of God instead of listening to himself rehearse the trials of this life. Now God enters the discussion. God has chosen to reveal Himself when we draw near to Him (see James 4:8). The psalmist hears these comforting and powerful truths from God. How precious it is when the Spirit of God whispers the truth of the Word of God into the heart of His hurting child.

To hold fast to someone entails cleaving to someone because of great love and being joined together. God is delineating the path to deliverance. The act of clinging to God is one of humble recognition: my inability to deliver myself, God's ability to deliver, and the desire of God to deliver. This is why I run to Him. There's also another facet here—one of love. I want to be with Him. He's not only able—He's desirable. To hold fast to Him in love means I am in the very near presence of God, not letting go because I understand what He has done and my heart swells with gratitude, devotion, and commitment to Him.

I'm not only delivered from something but also to something, and in this case, Someone! This is entirely and positionally relational. I desire Him because I recognize that He is who He says He is, so He will do what He says He will do. The promise of deliverance is nestled in the practice of holding fast to God in love. He will deliver me from this world and its struggles—to Himself! This deliverance often won't be how or when I think it should be, but He is the ultimate place and person of deliverance. Hold fast!

The word "protect" means to be inaccessibly on high. Several translations render the word protect as "set him securely on high" or "I will set him on high." His protection involves placing me out of the reach of evil. The rest of the verse continues, *"because He knows my name."* It's of great significance that the psalmist ties in the name of God as the Most High, *El Elyon*, from verses 1 and 9. He is above all things; everything is beneath Him. When I cling to Him in love, I'm made inaccessible to anything and anyone that would overwhelm me, because I am with the Most High. Nothing can touch me, because nothing can touch Him. Nothing can reach me, because nothing can reach Him, and I am with Him.

Consequently, when I know Him and understand who He is, I will run to Him. *Where else* would I go? (John 6:68) *Who else* is higher? If I don't run to Him for deliverance and protection, I've likely

"Lord, to whom shall we go? You have the words of eternal life" see John 6:68

forgotten who He is and failed to hold fast to Him in love.

Praise God! Even when I do fail, and my grip loosens, He never lets me go. The songwriter pens it well:

> *When I fear my faith will fail, Christ will hold me fast;*
> *When the tempter would prevail He will hold me fast.*
> *I could never keep my hold through life's fearful path;*
> > *For my love is often cold;*
> > *He must hold me fast.*[5]
> > (see Psalm 149:4, Jude 24)

---

5 Ada Habershon (190), "He Will Hold Me Fast," Hymnary.org, accessed May 15, 2023, https://hymnary.org/text/when_i_fear_my_faith_will_fail.

Personal Reflections

1. Write out Psalm 91:14

_____

_____

_____

_____

_____

2. To what/whom do I hold fast in love?

_____

_____

_____

_____

_____

3. How does pondering the truth that I am delivered *from* something *to* Someone challenge my functioning concept of deliverance?

_____

_____

_____

_____

_____

4. Because God's protection involves placing me out of reach of evil, what does this mean when sorrows, pains, and challenges come my way?

_____

_____

_____

_____

_____

5. Contemplate *El Elyon*. Consider His high protection and unfailing grip. Write a prayer of thankfulness for His protection and presence.

_____

_____

_____

_____

_____

Psalm 91:15

"When he calls to me,
I will answer him;
I will be with him in trouble;
I will rescue him and honor him."

SORROWS, FEARS, AGONIES, losses, and longings can tumultuously break my heart and leave me floundering. Where am I to go? Upon whom can I call and find actual help? God reaches into Psalm 91 with a promise of helpful response and rescue to those who call upon Him.

The kind of call referred to here is also used to refer to a beast crying out, or someone weeping. I can come broken and howling in pain to the Most High, the Almighty God. Thanks to Jesus, I have access to the throne room of heaven to find grace and mercy to help in time of need (see Hebrews 4:16). This access is remarkable, and God promises to answer the cry of my shattered heart. He hears me. I am not shouting sorrows and questions into empty space. The God of all glory bends His ear to me. Do I lift my voice to Him? All too often I weep and grieve in isolation from God. I rehash the struggles and enemies I'm facing and endeavor to concoct a plan. "*When he calls to me ...*" God is inviting me to a moment of intimate connection where I willingly expose the depths of my soul, call to Him, and wait for His answer.

As I press into His care with the depths of my need, He promises that He will answer. Like a mother who knows and hears the voice of her child, He will move to respond to my call. Because of who He is, I should long for and be willing to wait for His answer.

Notice that He doesn't state how He will answer. "*Call to me and I will answer you, and tell you great and hidden things that you have not known*" (Jeremiah 33:3, emphasis added). God's answer is beyond anything I could come up with on my own. I am the one charged with calling. He is the one promising to answer.

God doesn't do His listening from afar off. He doesn't simply send a messenger or shout across the chasm of our contrasting natures. He promises that when I call to Him, He will not withdraw but will instead press into me (see James 4:8). This is an astounding thought! All the heavy baggage: deep sorrows, anxieties, filthiness, weaknesses, failures, doubts, enemies, and sin-soaked motives of my heart are burdens of trouble He is *willing* and *wanting* to face *with* me. He promises, "*I will be with*

> God doesn't do His listening from afar off.

him in trouble." The psalmist reiterates the absolute reality of trouble, but he also reiterates the ultimate resource with which I can face times of trouble: the very presence of God! There is no distress capable of overwhelming God or causing trepidation within Him that could provoke His distance. Whatever I face, wherever I am, He, the Most High, who is my refuge (v. 9), will be with me (see Deuteronomy 31:6, 8; Hebrews 13:5).

God's promises are not finished. He says, "I *will rescue him and honor him.*" God has the power and plans to deliver me. It's tempting to define deliverance by my definitions. If the ultimate goal of God is to deliver me from trials, I might conclude that He has either failed or lied. Instead, His ultimate goal for my life is to put Himself on display in the best way possible. Deliverance will come—it just might not come in my time or my way, because He's going to do what is necessary to exalt Himself even in my suffering.

I must remember how far He allowed Jesus to suffer *and* what Jesus's suffering accomplished (see Isaiah 53:11). The most harrowing death was followed by the most glorious victory—the resurrection! Jesus begged for rescue (see Matthew 26:39), but He also continued entrusting Himself to the *One* who judges justly. Oh, Jesus was rescued! His rescue from the grave accomplished far more than a rescue from dying on the cross ever could. Because He lives, I can live. Look at what God accomplished with such anguish of soul, such agony of body, and such tormented sorrow! Christ did indeed suffer, yet what a glorious, eternal victory was won because of His submission to His Father, even as

He faced a brutal, unjust death. He left me an example to follow, so follow I will. I will entrust my soul to a faithful Creator while doing good (see 1 Peter 2:21–24, 4:19). The tempests of life, both its sorrows and victories, are platforms for gospel glory.

God doesn't deliver me and then leave me to flounder with sorrow that has no resolution. For what is rescue without resolution but purposeless loss? No, God's rescue is far more reaching than mere escape. His rescue involves eternal purposes that I can't even begin to fathom. However, if I could, I know I would crave such an outcome because it comes from a just Father's faithful hand. God invites me to rest in Him so that I don't miss the *only* rescue that can bring purpose and beauty even to my pain.

God will honor me when I call. He honors the fact that I have made Him my dwelling place and have called upon Him. He responds in eternally weighed measures to accomplish my deliverance. His response honors me. Consider this: the High King hears me, answers me, is with me, and rescues me. What honor indeed.

Personal Reflections

1. Write out Psalm 91:15.

_____

_____

_____

_____

_____

2. In what ways have I been weeping in isolation from God?

_____

_____

_____

_____

_____

3. Do I believe I cannot or should not come broken and needy before God? Why or why not?

_____

_____

_____

_____

_____

4. What thoughts, positive or negative, go through my mind when I read, "The tempests of life are platforms for gospel glory?" Am I defining deliverance by my definitions?

_____

_____

_____

_____

_____

5. Describe why it's astounding that the God of Glory bends His ear to me? How does this honor me?

_____

_____

_____

_____

_____

Psalm 91:16

> "With long life I will satisfy him
> and show him my salvation."

UPON READING THIS, my heart goes to the countless number of individuals whose lives have, by human standards, come to an "untimely" end. How many of them were faithful servants of God whose lives were "cut short"? Did God fail, or perhaps I should begin to question if those individuals didn't hold fast to Him in love and call upon Him? These would be erroneous conclusions. When I confine matters of eternity to moments in time, the plan of the eternal God will always conflict with my temporal understanding. There is no life *longer* than eternal. The pulsing desire of Jesus' true disciples is the fulfilled promise of eternal life with Christ. This present life simply cannot satisfy.

Every moment on this earth, from the heights of pleasure to the depths of despair, is fraught with the continual reminder of my frailty, my failures, and the finite realities that surround me. The deep ache of my soul recognizes that everything here leaves me wanting, empty, thirsty. God has promised something *better*, something *longer* than the limited time on this earth. When this timebound-life does indeed end, I will be going to my *longer* home, my eternal home. I will be satisfied! When granted entrance into heaven, I won't desire more time here, as He will *show me* His salvation. Oh, to see the intricate details of His plans and how my life intersected with those plans. It will be marvelous to finally experience the fullness of His salvation (see 1 Peter 1:3–9). One day, the terror of the night *will be* defeated, the arrow *will be* stopped, the pestilence *will be* eradicated, and the destruction *will be* restored! One day I will look into the face of the Most High, whom I have made my dwelling place, and I will forever dwell unhindered. He is going to do this work. Sin will lose its hold on me. I will no longer doubt and malign Him, for I will see Him as He is (see 1 John 3:2).

> *"...and the things of earth will grow strangely dim*
> *in the light of His glory and grace."*[6]

> *"But until then,*
> *my heart will go on singing,*
> *until then with joy I'll carry on.*
> *Until the day my eyes behold the Savior.*
> *Until the day God calls me home."*[7]

---

6 Helen Lemmel, "Turn Your Eyes upon Jesus," 1922, Hymns Illustrated, accessed April 21, 2023, https:// www.hymnsillustrated.com/Turn-Your-Eyes-upon-Jesus.
7 Carl Stuart Hamlen, "Until Then," 1958, Word Wise Hymns, accessed April 21, 2023, https://wordwisehymns.com/2013/08/09/until-then/.

Remaining in the very near presence of God now is so crucial. Psalm 91 reminds me that a foretaste of heaven is available to me amid desolation. While the world crumbles around me, I can be satisfied because my life is *longer*, and His salvation is available to me immediately. It's available here, now! I can watch with eternal anticipation to see how God will bring about His glory through something so tragic, so *seemingly* final. I'll see Him work out His perfection in the trials and sorrows of life, where it seems fear and death reign and rule.

I'll meet and hold my precious Tikvah, and with fullness of understanding, I will exalt the all-good, all-wise God who in His faithfulness took and withheld. I'll watch the transformative power of God take all sin and its consequences and utilize them for His glory and my good. These terrorizing realities are merely platforms upon which God exalts Himself and demonstrates His ability to eternally conquer. Therefore, I can be satisfied now. I can exalt Him now, not because of this life, but because of my God, who is at work in this life. Remember what He has said He will do:

- Deliver me (vv. 3, 14)
- Cover me (v. 4)
- Relieve my fear (vv. 5–7)
- Remove me from wrath (vv. 7–10)
- Protect me (vv. 3, 4, 7, 10, 14)
- Command His angels to guard me (vv. 11–12)
- Give me the victory (v. 13)
- Answer me (vv. 15)
- Be with me in trouble (v. 15)
- Rescue me (v. 15)
- Honor me (v. 15)
- Satisfy me with long life (v. 16)
- Show me his salvation (v. 16)

The Almighty, *El Shaddai*, will take the realities of this life and powerfully manipulate them to demonstrate who He is. I don't want to miss His glorious display because I'm frittering away on futile expectations that, when idolized, demote and trivialize the most desirable *One*. I don't want my pain to lose its purpose because I failed to run to *Jehovah*, the I Am, the eternal covenant-keeping God of steadfast love. I want to be satisfied *now*, because I'm thinking *longer*, looking higher, dwelling nearer, delving deeper, praying sooner, resting fuller, and in so doing finding myself in the shelter of the Most High while abiding in the shadow of the Almighty—the very near presence of God.

Think longer!

He is My Dwelling Place.

Personal Reflections

1. Write out Psalm 91:16.

_____

_____

_____

_____

_____

2. When life seems cut short, why is it erroneous to think that God failed or that faithful people weren't actually faithful?

_____

_____

_____

_____

_____

3. How can I experience a foretaste of eternal glory in the here and now?

_____

_____

_____

_____

_____

4. When I don't dwell in the very near presence of God, what do I lose? When I do dwell in the very near presence of God, what do I gain?

_____

_____

_____

_____

_____

5. As I leave Psalm 91, how am I going to actively remain in my dwelling place?

_____

_____

_____

_____

_____

6. Write out a prayer of praise to God for His shelter and commit to dwelling in His presence.

_____

_____

_____

_____

_____

Dear Reader,

WHILE SITTING IN that earlier-mentioned conference, the floodgates broke open. There I sat, reliving it all again. I didn't know I could cry any more tears. Where were they coming from? When would they stop? Indeed, they were coming from the depths of a heart broken by loss and shattered hopes. They were coming from a heart filled with questions about God, pain, good, and evil.

Perhaps as you've read this book your own floodgates have broken open, your own questions have throbbed, and your own fears have been exposed. I ache with you in your pain. I ache with you for what was, what is, what will never be, what might have been, and the fear of what will be. The anguish of soul is real, and it is appropriate to grieve (see Matthew 26:36–46; Hebrews 5:7–10). But don't forget, He will be with you in trouble (Psalm 91:15). He wants to know your sorrows, your questions, your fears. Take them to Him. Stay there, in the very near presence of *Elohim* (my God). Make the Lord your Dwelling Place.

I wish I could convey to you the depths of comfort God has provided through Psalm 91. There is *still* sadness. The loss is *still* real, but He is *still* God! So I can be still! As I dwell in the very near presence of *El Elyon* (the Most High), I am challenged to look higher and think longer. I pray you have also been encouraged, equipped, challenged, and comforted.

Look higher! Think longer, my friend.

All for Jesus, Christa Mielke, Psalm 73:25–26

CHRISTA MIELKE WAS rescued from her sin by her loving Lord through the faithful sharing of her grade school cousin. Upon her repentance, Jesus washed her clean for His glory and use. After a time of rebellion in her teen years, God lovingly chastened her back to His side. She is so grateful for His faithfulness to restore, confirm, strengthen, and establish her (1 Peter 5:10) and to call her into full-time service for His glory.

Christa is from Austin, Minnesota and enjoys serving alongside her husband, who is also her pastor. With three wonderful children in her home and one in heaven, being a wife and mother is her priority and delight. She considers serving alongside her husband in both family life and ministry a gracious gift from God. As a Homeschool Mom, she's amazed at the privilege of being entrusted with precious lives, and she's thankful for the grace and daily reminder that God would use a sinner to bring about His glory in the formation of young lives.

Knowing Jesus and proclaiming Him is Christa's heartbeat. Throughout sixteen years of ministry, God has continued to show Himself strong and given her many opportunities to serve Him. Christa is the Women's Ministry Steward at Grace Baptist, where she is actively involved in teaching and discipling women. She is passionate about the deep study of God's Word and treasures opportunities to share His truth with her children, individual women, her church, community, and at women's retreats or conferences. If Christa can be of help to you, please reach out via email to Christas6@gmail.com.

Printed in the USA
CPSIA information can be obtained
at www.ICGtesting.com
LVHW081748031123
762986LV00046B/1080

9 781486 624256